INSTA L.

101 *Must-Snap* Photo Ops in Los Angeles

Edited by **Dorie Bailey**

PROSPECT PARK BOOKS

Special thanks to our fabulous contributing editor Julianne Johnson for all her work on this book, as well as the lovely Emily Powers and Ellery McGregor for helping pull this project txogether.

Back cover credits (top left, clockwise): Veronica E. Lo (@buenobassets, p. 13), Paul Kadzielski (@mayorofla, p. 29), Chris Moynihan (@cmoynihan, p. 98), and Nazneen Shaik (@eazynazy, p. 71).

Prospect Park Books
2359 Lincoln Ave.
Altadena, CA 91001
www.prospectparkbooks.com

Table of Contents

A Note from the Editor.....3

NATURE.....3

CULTURE.....19

LANDMARKS.....39

ART & MURALS.....59

BUSINESSES.....79

Contributor Credits.....104
Index.....106

A NOTE FROM THE EDITOR @doriebee

SO HERE'S THE THING: Los Angeles, much like Instagram, is a vast and ever-changing landscape. Sometimes it feels like there's so much going on at any given moment that there's no *way* you'll ever catch up before the next big thing opens. Before you dig out your pitchforks and torches because I left out your favorite place, just know that I know that this book is not the end-all authority—it's more like a highlight reel of some of L.A.'s more permanant destinations worthy of your time and attention (and even these are subject to change, from when we upload to print to the exact moment your eyeballs are finishing this sentence).

If you scoff at the "touristy" nature of some of these places, trust me, I get it. But since when has playing tourist in your own city—especially the City of Angels—ever been a bad thing? Who knows, you might just discover your new favorite view of the city, or your next destination for a big Friday night out, or even the best new place to show your out-of-town friends. In all honesty, I'm not sure any book could ever capture the true scope of just how many unique, eye-catching, artistic, and delicious things are happening at any given moment in the L.A. area. I mean, what else would you expect from one of the most diverse cities in the country, not to mention one with a population larger than that of most states in the U.S.?

Insta L.A. is a book, not a living list of everything that L.A. has to offer, so I'd suggest following a couple of my favorite accounts for the best updates: **@discoverla** is always on top of what's going on around town, and **@lamag** posts highlights that will make anyone want to stay here forever and ever. Both showcase the amazing work of the thousands of Instagrammers who capture the beauty of Los Angeles every day, just like the real Instagrammers you're about to join on your trek to discover my 101 favorite locations—from the opulent Huntington Gardens shown on the right, to the dramatic Westin Bonaventure Hotel on the last page (the place that inspired this very book!).

You'll find a full list of contributing photographers at the end. Now go explore *Insta L.A.*!

Nature

THE HUNTINGTON LIBRARY, ART COLLECTIONS AND BOTANICAL GARDENS @emiok

With 120 acres of botanical goodness, an extensive art collection, and the drool-worthy Tea Room (not to mention the amazing gift shop), there's really no wrong way to take a great photo at the Huntington.

1151 Oxford Rd, San Marino, 91108

ABANDONED L.A. ZOO @ hannahmonica310

Mr. Brightside fans, your time has come. If you're looking for the animals, you'll have to go to the real zoo, but the graffiti-coated remnants of the old zoo are only a short hike away once you're in lovely Griffith Park.

4801 Griffith Park Dr, Los Angeles, 90027

@peiwayfarer **ARLINGTON GARDEN**

A wishing tree, rock labyrinth, native plants, and plenty of butterflies make this drought-tolerant garden a quaint spot just perfect for photos and picnicking. Also, check out the #forkintheroad, just up the street—it's pretty hard to miss.

275 Arlington Dr, Pasadena, 91105

ASCOT HILLS PARK @_alien.foto_

Arguably one of the best viewpoints in the city, this park offers some moderate hiking trails and plenty of backdrop. Try to go when the wildflowers are in bloom; it's really something else.

4371 Multnomah St, Los Angeles, 90032

@bon_mot_bot **BARNSDALL ART PARK**

Yet to snap the perfect L.A. sunset? Barnsdall's got you covered—just bring a blanket and watch the sky with a snack. Come early to check out the free onsite gallery and tour the gorgeous Frank Lloyd Wright Hollyhock House.

4800 Hollywood Blvd, Los Angeles, 90027

EATON CANYON WATERFALL @kbmangkeykeys

We can't guarantee a roaring waterfall (we *are* in a drought, after all), but the easy hike and family-friendly Nature Center still make for a fun time. For more advanced trails, try Henniger Flats or Mount Wilson for a stellar view.

1750 N Altadena Dr, Pasadena, 91107

@britt_p **ECHO PARK LAKE**

Take a spin on a pedal boat and soak up all the oasis vibes this peaceful park offers. And do say hello to the Lady of the Lake, sculpted by Ada May Sharpless in 1934.

751 Echo Park Ave, Los Angeles, 90026

EL MATADOR STATE BEACH @lucaspassmore

This dreamy beach is one of Malibu's best, complete with a healthy scattering of pose-perfect rocks, plenty of picnic tables, and a picturesque staircase down to the sand.

32350 Pacific Coast Hwy, Malibu, 90265

@lolagoeswest **EXPOSITION PARK ROSE GARDEN**

More than 200,000 rose bushes fill this seven-acre garden, but that's just the beginning—Exposition Park is also home to the Natural History Museum, California Science Center, California African American Museum, and the Coliseum (see p. 49).

701 State Dr, Los Angeles, 90037

MANHATTAN BEACH PIER @kristina_marshall

You can't go wrong with a pic of the pier—above or below, midday or at sunset. Just be sure to keep an eye on the tide!

Manhattan Beach Pier, Manhattan Beach, 90266

@buenobassets **ROSIE'S DOG BEACH**

Sure, you could visit any one of L.A.'s many beaches, but because this is the only designated off-leash dog beach in the region, we recommend you start here—especially if you're looking to start a lucrative Insta career for your pup.

5000 E Ocean Blvd, Long Beach, 90803

RUNYON CANYON @damnitrj

Yes, everyone and their mother has done this hike—but the view can't be beat. Brace yourself for the throngs of beautiful people, super-cute dogs, and opportunistic photo shoots happening up and down the route.

2000 N Fuller Ave, Los Angeles, 90046

@waifwanderer **SECRET SWING ELYSIAN PARK**

A short but steep climb up a rather nondescript hill will reward you with the best seat in the house (tree?) for a fantastic view of the city—but always swing with caution!

929 Academy Road, Los Angeles, 90012

TONGVA PARK @axelecastilhos

More than six acres of drought-resistant plants from all over the world, sculptures, bridges, a play area for kids, and more make Tongva Park a great daytime stop if you're exploring Santa Monica.

1615 Ocean Ave, Santa Monica, 90401

@gabbyfeola **VENICE BEACH**

Can storied Venice Beach really be defined in a single category? We decided on Nature, but between the boardwalk, skate park, abundance of street art (#venicesuites!), and everything else going on, you'll be sufficiently busy with things to do and see.

1800 Ocean Front Walk, Venice, 90291

VENICE CANALS @tomelkon

Hunt for your dream home (respectfully, as this is a residential area) in style as you wander around the quaint canals and bridges of this historic district.

200 Linnie Canal, Venice, 90291

DODGER STADIUM @graysonpropst

The largest-capacity baseball stadium in the world is rich with history and a lot of civic pride. Try to make it to a game—sunset at the stadium and a Dodger dog is a tough combo to beat.

1000 Vin Scully Ave, Los Angeles, 90012

Culture

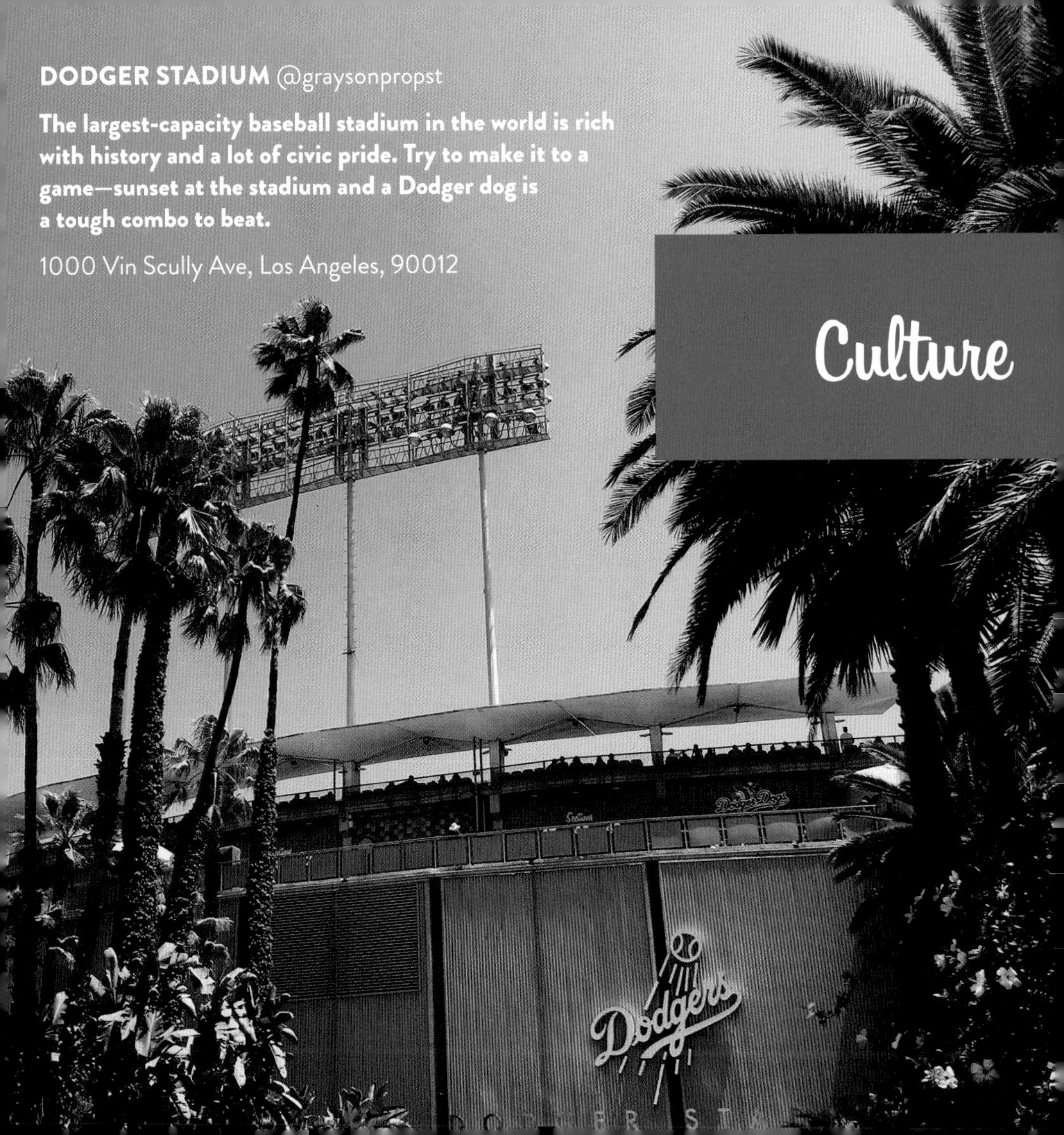

THE BROAD @btswpdb

You'll need a reservation in advance for a guaranteed shot in Yayoi Kusama's #infinityroom, but even without one, the permanent collection at the Broad (that's pronounced "brode") is well worth your time—and admission is free!

221 S Grand Ave, Los Angeles, 90012

@itsjustinbitch **CAFAM**

The Craft and Folk Art Museum along Miracle Mile is hard to miss with that eye-popping paint job. Head inside for creative rotating exhibits, hands-on workshops, and a total gem of a shop.

5814 Wilshire Blvd, Los Angeles, 90036

CALTECH @mmmols

You can almost feel yourself growing smarter as you stroll through the grounds of this historic institution. Check caltech.edu for info about the campus architecture tour, and grab lunch at the legendary Pie 'n Burger down the street for a bonus photo op.

1200 E California Blvd, Pasadena, 91125

@alexc43 **THE CINERAMA DOME**

The dome might be a little dressed up, depending on the latest movie showing, but this classic piece of L.A. history—built in only sixteen weeks—was artfully restored in 2002 and is now part of the ArcLight Hollywood.

6360 Sunset Blvd, Los Angeles, 90028

THE GETTY @zheo_verticies

Standing tall over Los Angeles, the Getty is just as stunning on the outside as its collections are on the inside. Don't miss the bougainvilleas or the sculpture gardens, either.

1200 Getty Center Dr, Los Angeles, 90049

@blondiemonster **HERITAGE SQUARE MUSEUM**

Just off the 110 freeway, this living history museum is only open Friday-Sunday, but the ornate Victorian houses they've carefully restored are most definitely worth the guided tour.

3800 Homer St, Los Angeles, 90031

HOLLYWOOD BOWL @kimberlydhicks

This legendary venue has hosted countless musical icons since its opening in 1922, and the various Sing-A-Long performances and summer concerts by the L.A. Philharmonic are favorites of music-lovers from all over the world.

2301 N Highland Ave, Los Angeles, 90068

@nickpes **HOLLYWOOD FOREVER CEMETERY**

Besides hosting concerts and film screenings, the cemetery and its beautiful mausoleum are the final resting place of a number of notables, including Rudolph Valentino, Judy Garland, and George Harrison.

6000 Santa Monica Blvd, Los Angeles, 90038

KOREAN BELL OF FRIENDSHIP @roundtripweekend

This seventeen-ton bell is only rung four times a year, and was sent by the Republic of Korea in 1976 to celebrate America's bicentennial. The neighboring Point Fermin Park is also worthy of a stop.

3601 S Gaffey St, San Pedro, 90731

@mayorofla **L.A. PUBLIC LIBRARY**

Between the hundreds of thousands of printed volumes, photographs, and digital media, and the awe-inspiring art and architecture of the building itself, the free guided tours are the best way to fully experience the Central Library.

630 W 5th St, Los Angeles, 90071

L.A. THEATRE @ilovemylife75

The Los Angeles Theatre is one of the most lavish landmarks in the city—see it and other nearby historical buildings up close and personal on an L.A. Conservancy walking tour (Saturday mornings, check laconservancy.org).

615 S Broadway, Los Angeles, 90014

@tamara_samira **THE LIGHTHOUSE CAFE**

The Lighthouse Cafe was a star in its own right long before *La La Land*, celebrating jazz and other great live music since 1949. Poke your head in after you snap a photo and you might just thank us for your new favorite Sunday brunch spot.

30 Pier Ave, Hermosa Beach, 90254

LITTLE TOKYO @shintani

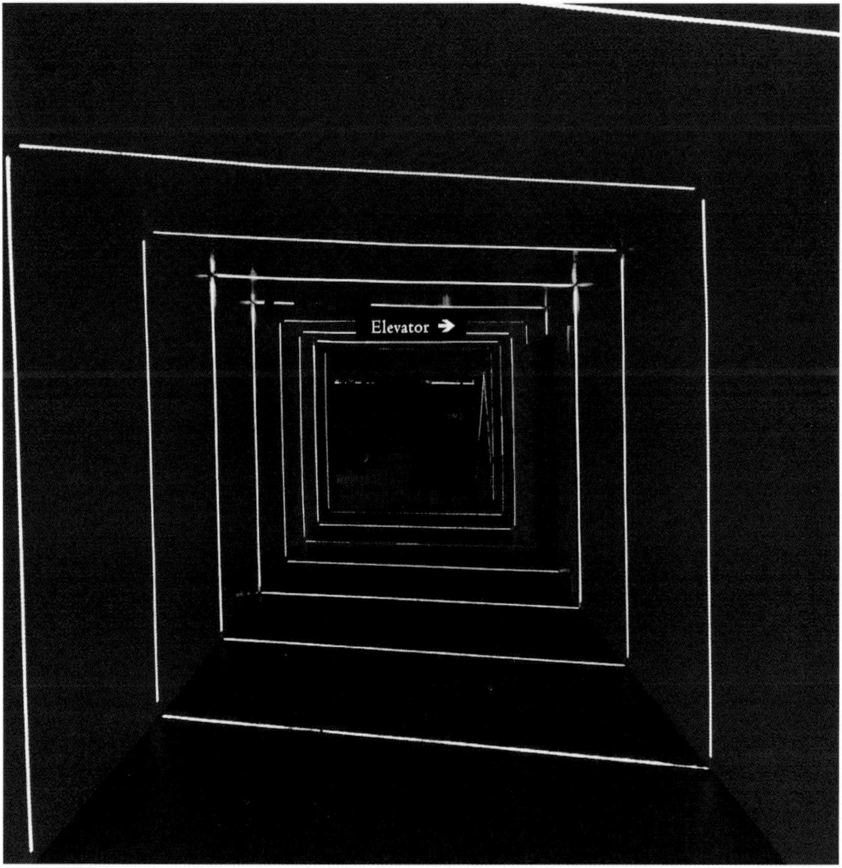

You might need a whole day to fully explore Little Tokyo—so many restaurants, museums, shops, and gardens, so little time! Pictured is *Portal* by artist Akiko Yamashita (@akikoyamashita3d), found at Weller Court.

123 Astronaut Ellison S Onizuka St, Los Angeles, 90012

@kristaaablair **MUSEUM OF NEON ART**

The engaging exhibits here may come and go, but the coveted bathroom selfie at the MONA will never go out of style. Don't worry, there's one in the men's room, too!

216 S Brand Blvd, Glendale, 91204

NORTON SIMON MUSEUM @danly

You'll want to set aside some time to fully explore this treasure trove of an art collection. As you do, feel free to pose your heart out in the impressive sculpture garden and alongside Edgar Degas's *Little Dancer*.

411 W Colorado Blvd, Pasadena, 91105

@beteille **OLVERA STREET**

Peruse the shops and indulge in some of the best taquitos in the city (that's saying something!) as you explore one of L.A.'s oldest and most richly historical areas.

Olvera St, Los Angeles, 90012

PASADENA PLAYHOUSE @prettyinpasadena

The official state theater of California has a long and storied history, graceful architecture, and a jazzy crosswalk out front to boot. For a double-whammy photo op, visit on a Tuesday—Trejo's Cantina is right next door, and the tacos are tasty.

39 S El Molino Ave, Pasadena, 91101

@christinlthieme **SANTA ANITA PARK**

The history and architecture of this racetrack are well worth taking the free weekend *Seabiscuit* tour, and you can sit trackside and watch the horses practice during racing season while you eat one of L.A.'s best secret bargain breakfasts at Clockers' Corner.

285 Huntington Dr, Arcadia, 91007

WALT DISNEY CONCERT HALL @gabri.in.the.city

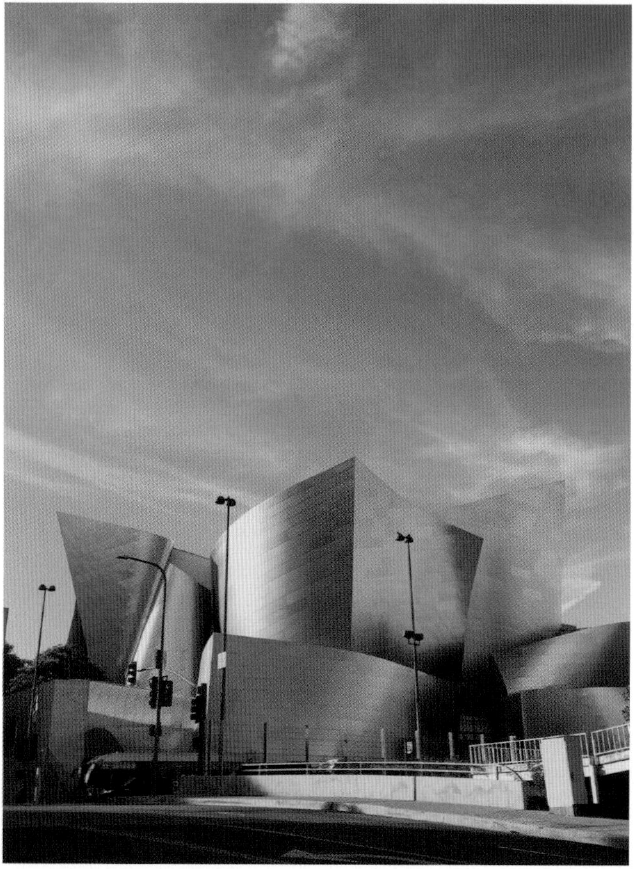

Thank you, Frank Gehry, for this iconic silhouette! Check laphil.com for info about venue tours (definitely worth your while), and if you can, stage a mini photo shoot in the Blue Ribbon Garden.

111 S Grand Ave, Los Angeles, 90012

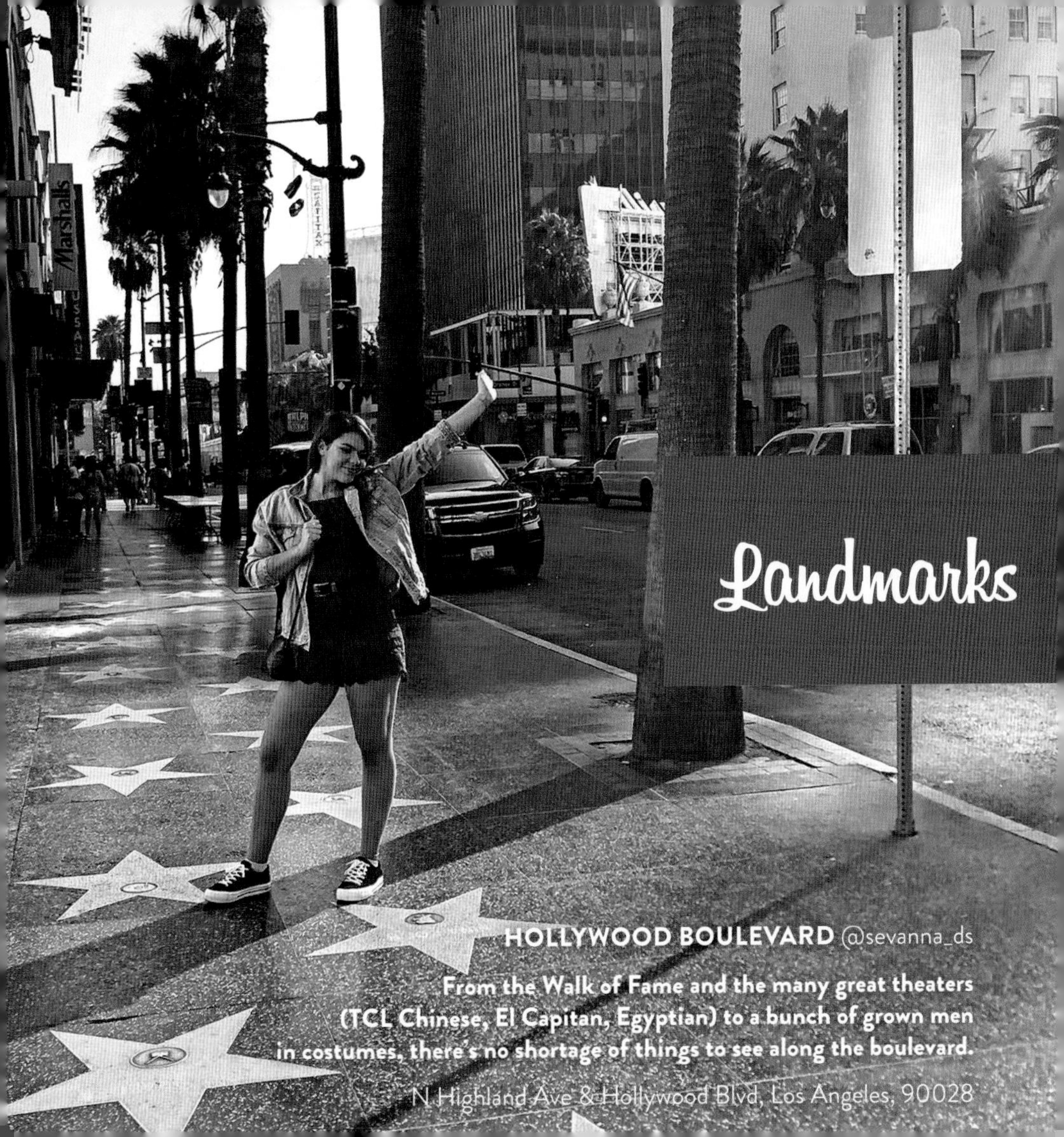

Landmarks

HOLLYWOOD BOULEVARD @sevanna_ds

From the Walk of Fame and the many great theaters (TCL Chinese, El Capitan, Egyptian) to a bunch of grown men in costumes, there's no shortage of things to see along the boulevard.

N Highland Ave & Hollywood Blvd, Los Angeles, 90028

ANGELS FLIGHT RAILWAY @smallforwardmusic

With more than 100 million completed rides and counting, Angels Flight charges only a buck for the short "flight" up (or down) Bunker Hill in the circa-1905 cars of one of the world's shortest funiculars.

350 S Grand Ave, Los Angeles, 90071

@insta.otakar **BEVERLY HILLS SIGN**

There's lots to see and do in the ol' 90210, from a stop at the Beverly Hills sign to window shopping on Rodeo Drive. Be sure to, like, totally pause at the stop sign at Elevado Avenue & North Hillcrest Road to fully embrace your inner Cher Horowitz.

9390 N Santa Monica Blvd, Beverly Hills, 90210

BRADBURY BUILDING @anniechen.nyc

Odds are you recognize this stunning 1893 building from any number of movies or TV shows. If you're into all things spooky, you might want to read up on exactly how the oldest commercial building in the area came to be.

304 S Broadway, Los Angeles, 90013

@kh_jesse0626 **CAPITOL RECORDS BUILDING**

Did you know that the red light at the top of the spire spells out HOLLYWOOD in morse code? While you're there, check out the lovingly restored *Hollywood Jazz* mural by Richard Wyatt Jr. along the south wall.

1750 Vine St, Los Angeles, 90028

CHINATOWN CENTRAL PLAZA @________leri

Besides the vintage architecture, touristy shops, and great food, L.A.'s Chinatown is now also home to a variety of art galleries, and it's easily accessible via the Metro Gold Line. You can't visit without trying your luck at the wishing fountain!

943 N Broadway, Los Angeles, 90012

@okarol **COLORADO STREET BRIDGE**

There's just something magical about this historic bridge at dusk—just ask Ryan Gosling and Emma Stone. Perhaps even better are the winding Arroyo Seco trails that run directly below it.

504 W Colorado Blvd, Pasadena, 91105

EASTERN COLUMBIA BUILDING @see_j_now

If you think the entryway is amazing, just wait till you see the rest of this art deco beauty. Check page 30 for more info on the L.A. Conservancy walking tours, which include this building and more.

849 S Broadway, Los Angeles, 90014

@oliver_kowalsky **GRIFFITH OBSERVATORY**

The incomparable view, Kenneth Kendall's *Rebel Without a Cause* monument, the Tesla coil, and the planetarium shows are just a few of the things you'll find up here. And admission has been free since 1935, courtesy of Mr. Griffith J. Griffith.

2800 E Observatory Rd, Los Angeles, 90027

HOLLYWOOD SIGN @_cagataysevil

You can see this legendary sign from all over the city, but if you're looking for a picture like this, you'll have to hike one of the trails that will get you closer—a little online research will help you pick which one to take.

3160 Canyon Lake Dr, Los Angeles, 90068

@bertosolis **L.A. MEMORIAL COLISEUM**

The recently renamed United Airlines Memorial Coliseum is home to the USC Trojans football team. The stadium has also hosted numerous musical performances and the summer Olympics twice (and will again in 2028).

3911 S Figueroa St, Los Angeles, 90037

OLD TOWN PASADENA @periencinas

Visit Viola Frey's *Kneeling Man with Hammer* (above), the famed Castle Green, or the many side streets for more shops, eating, and photo-shoot-ready exposed brick than you can shake a selfie stick at. Christensen Alley is a great place to start!

Smith Alley, Pasadena, 91105

@yourplaceofbirth **ORIGINAL FARMERS MARKET**

Built in 1934, the OG L.A. farmers' market is still serving up amazing food, fresh groceries, novelty hot sauces, live music performances, and personality galore. If you're looking for modernity and chain stores, head to The Grove—it's right next door.

6333 W 3rd St, Los Angeles, 90036

PASADENA CITY HALL @npphotog

More than just Pawnee City Hall, this Pasadena gem is noted for its graceful architecture and many wedding photo shoots on the front steps. Catch it at golden hour or sunset and you'll be in for a real treat.

100 Garfield Ave, Pasadena, 91101

@poindexterity **QUEEN ANNE COTTAGE**

This gabled, turreted cottage is found deep in the heart of the lush Los Angeles County Arboretum and Botanic Garden— but watch out for preening peacocks!

107 S Baldwin Ave, Arcadia, 91007

THE QUEEN MARY @manicpixietravel

Since Her Majesty retired from the seas in 1967, this living landmark is now home to a museum, fine dining, and a popular hotel, which may or may not be haunted....

1126 Queens Hwy, Long Beach, 90802

@melissahockings **SANTA MONICA PIER**

A solar-powered ferris wheel, carnival games, all kinds of tasty treats (hello, funnel cake!), and even an educational aquarium await you at this destination pier, originally opened in 1909.

200 Santa Monica Pier, Santa Monica, 90401

SPADENA HOUSE @findinglostangeles

Who can resist a photo in front of this storybook masterpiece? Also known as the Witch's House, this quirky structure is actually a private home, so please be respectful of the property.

516 Walden Dr, Beverly Hills, 90210

@julianne.jc **UNION STATION**

You've seen this 1939 train station in tons of movies and TV shows over the years (*Blade Runner*, *The Dark Knight Rises*, and *Seabiscuit*, to name just a few). A mix of art deco, streamline moderne, and mission revival architecture, it's one of L.A.'s jewels.

800 N Alameda St, Los Angeles, 90012

VENICE BEACH SIGN @nancygordy

While we're all for embracing the full experience of photographing this iconic sign, please be safe when posing in the middle of the street. That crosswalk is there for a reason!

Pacific Ave & Windward Ave, Venice, 90291

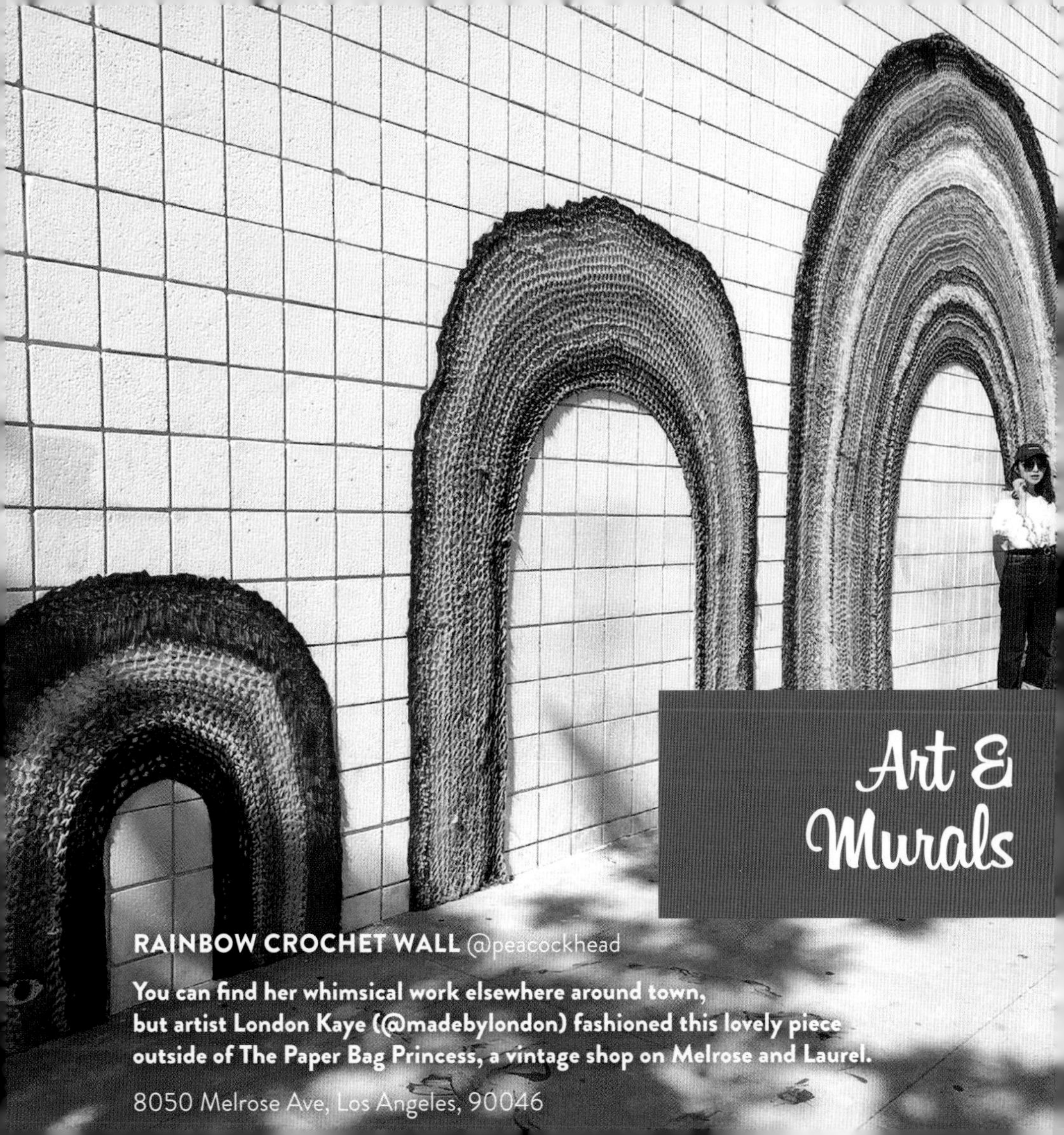

Art & Murals

RAINBOW CROCHET WALL @peacockhead

You can find her whimsical work elsewhere around town, but artist London Kaye (@madebylondon) fashioned this lovely piece outside of The Paper Bag Princess, a vintage shop on Melrose and Laurel.

8050 Melrose Ave, Los Angeles, 90046

ANGEL WINGS @wanderlust.portraits

Artist Colette Miller (@colettemillerwings)'s Global Angel Wings Project has spread all over the world, but there are quite a few throughout L.A. See colettemiller.com for a full list of locations, and go out there and snap them all!

2303 Miramar St, Los Angeles, 90057

@teresa.ctw **ASSEMBLY LOS ANGELES**

This fun upside-down/backwards typography adorns the wall of Assembly Los Angeles, a clothing store on Melrose. Check the #assemblylosangeles tag for more examples of how it looks IRL.

7977 Melrose Ave, Los Angeles, 90046

CALIFORNIA DREAMIN' MURAL @charlie_dog_in_LA

If you're dreaming of a perfect mural backdrop, the signature typography of Ricardo Gonzalez (@itsaliving) on the side of the Chinese Laundry building is exactly what you need.

3485 La Cienega Blvd, Los Angeles, 90016

@tinahli **DOTS CAFE WALL**

Some days you just have to
create your own *sunshine.*

This colorful mural by Geoff Gouveia (@geoffgouveia) adorns the outside of Dots Cafe & Bakery in Pasadena. Inside you'll find some seriously gorgeous wallpaper to rival it. Be sure to try a cupcake or two while you're there.

3819 E Colorado Blvd, Pasadena, 91107

ELLIOTT SMITH MURAL @iansotomay

Though half of the original mural that graced the cover of his *Figure 8* album is now gone, Elliott Smith fans still come here to pay their respects and celebrate the life of the late singer.

4334 Sunset Blvd, Los Angeles, 90029

@theprinceandthep **GIRLS TOUR WALL**

By far one of L.A.'s most famous murals, the #girlstour wall on the side of Sorella Boutique is the millennial-pink backdrop of your dreams.

7829 Melrose Ave, Los Angeles, 90046

HERMOSA BEACH MURALS @batuhantinar

The #17thstreetmuralhouse has an Angel Wings, but even cooler is the Hermosa Beach Murals Project; they're installing one new mural a year through 2020. Check out hermosamurals.org for locations; this is *Key of C* by John Pugh (@artofjohnpugh).

1007 Hermosa Ave & 11th Court, Hermosa Beach, 90254

@amalayy_ **LACMA LAMPS**

The museum itself should definitely be on your list, but the lamps alone draw tons of visitors. You can thank Chris Burden for this legendary L.A. photo location—*Urban Light* is one of the most photographed spots in all of Southern California.

5905 Wilshire Blvd, Los Angeles, 90036

MADE IN L.A. WALL @lexilopez22

Cisco Home, an L.A.-based sustainable furniture company, proudly proclaims its "Made in L.A." status on the side of its building. And now you can, too!

8025 Melrose Ave, Los Angeles, 90046

@skyeautumnwellness **MICHELTORENA HEART STAIRS**

There are tons of great #secretstairs throughout L.A., but these in particular are one of the most recognizable in the city, thanks to the original idea and upkeep by local artist Corinne Carrey (@corinnecarrey).

3400 Sunset Blvd, Los Angeles, 90026

MONDRIAN WALL @salinamendozaart

One of the coolest craft stores in L.A., Artist & Craftsman Supply's Mid-City location rocks this impressive storefront. Is that a Banksy or just a copycat?

1660 S La Cienega Blvd, Los Angeles, 90035

@eazynazy **MOSAIC TILE HOUSE**

Only open on Saturdays for free tours, this captivating weekend project-turned-large-scale art piece is the work of artists Cheri Pann and Gonzalo Duran—see cheripann.com for more, and call ahead to reserve a tour spot!

1116 Palms Blvd, Venice, 90291

OUTSIDEIN MURAL @keeganmdunn

Created by legendary street artist RISK (aka Kelly Graval, @riskrock) at ArtCenter College of Design as part of its OUTSIDEIN exhibition, this wall of color is guaranteed to brighten your feed.

950 S Raymond Ave, Pasadena, 91105

@gamzeesariyar **PAUL SMITH PINK WALL**

It's the #paulsmithpinkwall—need we say more? Luckily for you, this L.A. staple rarely strays from the Pepto-pink hue seen above, and it makes for a great photo backdrop 24/7/365.

8221 Melrose Ave, Los Angeles, 90046

SCREEN AT WILSHIRE GRAND CENTER @smaddielope

Korean artist Do Ho Suh's captivating piece *Screen* in the InterContinental Los Angeles Downtown's lobby is actually made of 85,000 tiny stacked figures—search #dohosuh for closeups and more about his amazing work.

935 W 7th St, Los Angeles, 90017

@macdaddymarmar **RETNA WALL WEST HOLLYWOOD**

Just one of RETNA (aka Marquis Lewis, @retna)'s many walls around town, this blue beauty is found at the West Hollywood Library, where you'll also find walls by Shepard Fairey (@obeygiant) and Kenny Scharf (@kennyscharf).

625 N San Vicente Blvd, West Hollywood, 90069

TRIFORIUM @jason_zyx

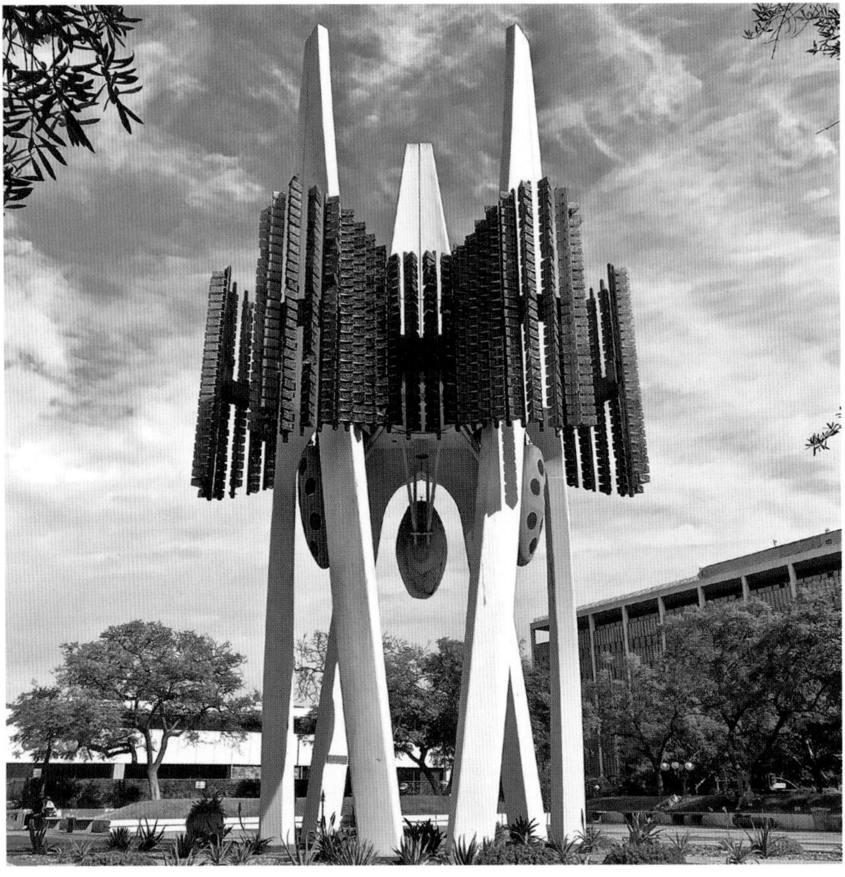

Artist Joseph Young's sixty-foot polyphonoptic tower has stood tall in L.A. for more than forty years. Once mocked and maligned, it has recently been brought back to life thanks to the Triforium Project.

Fletcher Bowron Square, N Main St, Los Angeles, 90012

@melbrods **VENICE PRIDE LIFEGUARD TOWER**

Originally created by artist Patrick Marston and husband Michael Brunt to commemorate #venicepride, this powerful paint job is now preserved indefinitely as the Bill Rosendahl Memorial Lifeguard Tower.

Brooks Ave & Oceanfront Walk, Venice, 90291

WATTS TOWERS @ginger_drew

Simon Rodia built these towers, also known as *Nuestro Pueblo*, by hand between 1921 and 1955 with found objects and scrap materials. LACMA began restoring the site in 2017, and limited tours are still being offered while that project is underway.

1727 E 107th St, Los Angeles, 90002

GRAND CENTRAL MARKET @ayceofspade

We'll let you discover the #frontierworks neon light wall for yourself. Just know that this century-old food hall has one of the best assortments of eating in the city, all located under one conveniently photogenic roof.

317 S Broadway, Los Angeles, 90013

Businesses

ACE HOTEL @sara_diamond

From the rooftop pool and "Jesus Saves" sign to the fabulous carpet and lighting in the powder room, you simply can't go wrong with a stop at the Ace DTLA. Major bonus points for the stunningly restored United Artists Theatre next door.

929 S Broadway, Los Angeles, 90015

 THE AMERICANA

The trendier neighbor of the Glendale Galleria, this outdoor shopping center has the faux-folksy, fantasy-small-town look of its sibling The Grove, complete with a trolley, movie theaters, fountain shows, and a vast choice of eateries.

889 Americana Way, Glendale, 91210

ANGEL CITY BREWERY @nicpitre

There's much more to Angel City than house-brewed beers on tap—the historic building in the Arts District is covered in graffiti and wall art, and it offers daily tours, board games and cards for patrons, and a rotating selection of food trucks.

216 S Alameda St, Los Angeles, 90012

@daniellellombard **THE BEVERLY HILLS HOTEL**

The Beverly Hills Hotel—rocking the Instagram-friendly millennial-pink and green color scheme, no less—is one place in L.A. that's always ripe for the picking. Who doesn't love a good banana-leaf background?

9641 Sunset Blvd, Beverly Hills, 90210

BURLINGTON ARCADE @elisabetstyles

Just as charming as the real London arcade of the same name, this pastel destination is home to shops, cafes, and, naturally, a picture-perfect red phone booth.

380 S Lake Ave, Pasadena, 91101

@cmog808 **CANTER'S DELI**

The home of classic corned beef, matzo ball soup, celebrity sightings, and more. What would a drive down Fairfax be without the comforting sight of the Canter's sign keeping watch over the city?

419 N Fairfax Ave, Los Angeles, 90036

CLIFTON'S REPUBLIC @jorgeshotthis

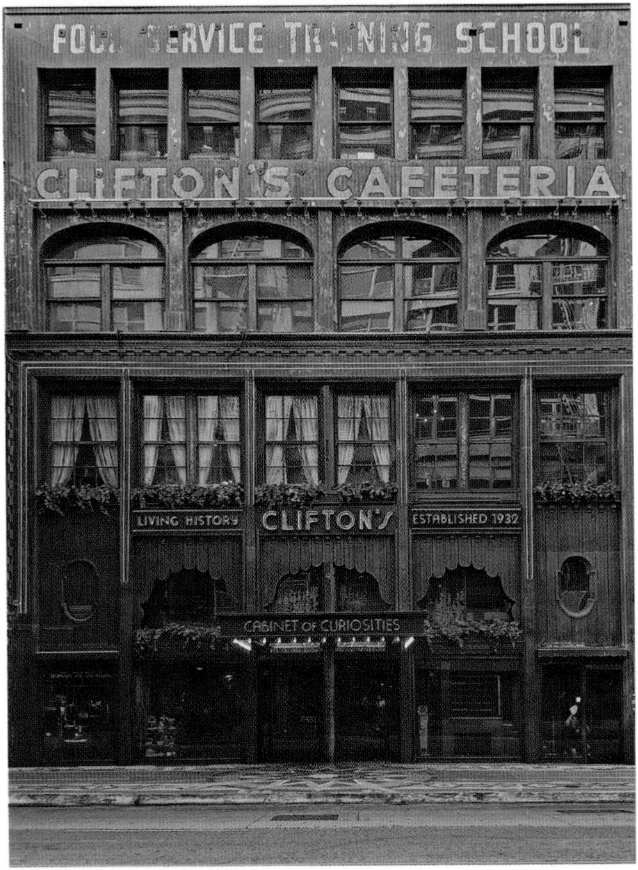

If the giant Coastal Redwood that greets you upon entry doesn't impress, perhaps the rest of Clifton's five floors of dining and drinking (like the secret tiki bar—it's a must-see) can convince you that it's one of the most unique spots in the city.

648 S Broadway, Los Angeles, 90014

@claireschwrz **FAIR OAKS PHARMACY**

The perfectly pastel South Pasadena staple is home to an actual pharmacy, a fun retail space, and a delightfully vast menu of both modern and old-fashioned treats—ten bucks says you can't finish the twelve-pound ice cream sundae!

1526 Mission St, South Pasadena, 91030

FLOWER DISTRICT @ppaulyo

With such a huge variety of colorful plants and flowers at this massive flower market, you're bound to discover something exciting. But come early—the good stuff sells out!

766 Wall St, Los Angeles, 90014

@alisonkorth **HIDDEN TREASURES**

Just imagine how fabulous you'd look perched in this chair! Vintage clothes, antiques, and an assortment of oddities make this a great stop for any dedicated and thrifty explorer.

154 S Topanga Canyon Blvd, Topanga, 90290

HIGHLAND PARK BOWL @date.the.city

The oldest bowling alley in L.A. certainly looks it from the outside, but inside you'll find a jaw-droppingly gorgeous restoration of the original space—including the exposed pin-racking machines and an awesome light fixture over the bar.

5621 N Figueroa St, Los Angeles, 90042

@irisfigs **IN-N-OUT**

From seasoned veterans to first-time indulgers, everyone snaps these beautiful buns at least once. In-N-Out began life in Baldwin Park in 1948, and the Burbank replica of that original tiny burger stand makes for a great photo, too.

761 N 1st St, Burbank, 91502

THE LAST BOOKSTORE @leeteaandpoetry

An L.A. institution, The Last Bookstore is packed with new and used books, records, and gifts. The incredible upstairs area houses art installations and photo ops aplenty.

453 S Spring St, Los Angeles, 90013

@elizabethpodlesnik **LINE LA'S OPENAIRE**

Formerly Roy Choi's Commissary, Openaire is the latest restaurant to bloom in this gorgeous greenhouse space at the LINE hotel in Koreatown. The menu and chef might have changed, but it's still a top-notch spot for a perfect shot (and a great meal!).

3515 Wilshire Boulevard, 2nd Floor, Los Angeles, 90010

MELROSE TRADING POST @ajquon

This is one of L.A.'s great flea markets, where you'll find vintage clothes, art, and furniture, live music, and yes, even some celebs. It runs every Sunday at Fairfax High School, and proceeds go to the Greenway Arts Alliance and student programs for the school.

7850 Melrose Ave, Los Angeles 90046

@chartie **MOONLIGHT ROLLERWAY**

Besides having a great carpet, the Moonlight Rollerway has appeared in many films, TV shows, and music videos. As an extra treat, you can hear the Rollerway's longtime owner, Dominic Cangelosi, play live organ music for skating on Tuesday nights.

5110 San Fernando Rd, Glendale, 91204

NEON RETRO ARCADE @sailorsushi

Need to beef up the vintage aesthetic of your feed? Look no further than the Neon Retro Arcade, where you can test your skills on more than fifty classic game and pinball machines for one flat fee.

28 S Raymond Ave, Pasadena, 91105

@mjtraynor **NOMAD LOS ANGELES**

Be sure to blow a kiss to the fabulous ceiling on your way into the hotel, and don't miss the opportunity for a selfie with this historic 1923 building's bank-vault door, which now leads to the bathrooms downstairs.

649 S Olive St, Los Angeles, 90014

RANDY'S DONUTS @cmoynihan

Yes, the giant donut is reason enough to pay Randy's a visit, but its famously handmade treats are the real star of the show. Better yet, make like fashion icon Harry Styles and pair a classic glazed with one of Randy's cozy gray hoodies.

805 W Manchester Blvd, Inglewood, 90301

@caitlinmiyako **REPUBLIQUE**

One of the best brunch spots in town, Republique occupies a gorgeous structure built by Charlie Chaplin in 1928. The French cuisine is as impressive as the space. Reservations recommended!

624 S La Brea Ave, Los Angeles, 90036

ROSE BOWL FLEA MARKET @theboldandvibrant

Despite the crowds and heat, it's worth hitting this iconic flea market at least once. Pro tip: If the admission price is too steep for you, Pasadena City College's flea market is free—the Rose Bowl's is the second Sunday of the month, and PCC's is the first.

1001 Rose Bowl Dr, Pasadena, 91103

@rebeccakooking **SANTA MONICA FARMERS MARKET**

The L.A. area has a seemingly endless list of great farmers markets, but the famous Santa Monica ones (four in total) are where you'll find some of the best colors, aromas, and tastes in the country.

250 Arizona Ave, Santa Monica, 90401

SMORGASBURG L.A. @foodie_mary

Head downtown to Smorgasburg every Sunday for dozens of photo-ready (and obviously super tasty!) food and drink options, as well as other rotating vendors and pop-ups.

787 S Alameda St, Los Angeles, 90021

@doriebee **WESTIN BONAVENTURE HOTEL**

L.A.'s largest hotel is certainly a sight to behold. Be sure to take one of the circular glass elevators up to the revolving BonaVista Lounge on the 34th floor—there's a plaque next to each one detailing its many film appearances.

404 S Figueroa St, Los Angeles, 90071

Contributor Credits

AJ Quon, @ajquon, p. 94
Alejandra Nunez, @ilovemylife75, p. 30
Alex Carillo, @alexc43, p. 23
Alexis Lopez, @lexilopez22, adventureswithlex22.wordpress.com, p. 68
Alison Korth, @alisonkorth, alisonkorth.com, p. 89
Amal Abshir, @amalayy_, p. 67
Andrew Park, @ayceofspade, aycecreative.com, p. 79
Annie Chen, @anniechen.nyc, anniechen.nyc, p. 42
Axele Castilhos, @axelecastilhos, p. 16
Ayelet Ifrah, @peacockhead, p. 59
Batuhan Tinar, @batuhantinar, p. 66
Brian Wang, @btswpdb, p. 20
Brittaney Parbs, @britt_p, p. 9
Cagatay Sevil, @_cagataysevil, p. 48
Caitlin Taylor, @caitlinmiyako, caitlinmiyako.com, p. 99
Carlos Juarez, @see_j_now, p. 46
Charline Tie, @chartie, p. 95
Chris Moynihan, @cmoynihan, p. 98
Christian Moraga, @cmog808, p. 85
Christin Thieme, @christinlthieme, christinlthieme.com, p. 37
Christopher Shintani, @shintani, shintaniphotography.com, p. 32
Claire Schwartz, @claireschwrz, p. 87
Dan Ly, @danly, p. 34
Daniel Martin, @yourplaceofbirth, theplaceofbirthsock.com, p. 51
Danielle Lombard, @daniellellombard, daniellelombard.com, p. 83
Dara Adeeyo, @lolagoeswest (photo: Deborah Ni), lolagoeswest.com, p. 11
Darra Stone, @manicpixietravel, p. 54
Dorie Bailey, @doriebee, p. 103
Drew Kraft, @ginger_drew, drewkraft.com, p. 78
Elisabet Mascorro, @elisabetstyles, elisabetstyles.com, p. 84
Elizabeth Podlesnik, @elizabethpodlesnik, elizabethpodlesnik.com, p. 93
Emily Okada, @emiok, emilyokada.com, p. 3
Eric Beteille, @beteille, pedestrianphotographer.com, p. 35
Eric Garcetti, @mayorofla (photo: Paul Kadzielski), lamayor.org, p. 29
Finding Lost Angeles, @findinglostangeles (photo: Nate Hennagin), findinglostangeles.com, p. 56
Gabriela Feola, @gabbyfeola, p. 17
Gabriella Trepasso, @gabri.in.the.city, everywheretravelkit.com, p. 38
Galen Jee, @npphotog, p. 52
Gamze Sariyar, @gamzeesariyar, p. 73
Grayson Propst, @graysonpropst, graysonpropst.com, p. 19
Hannah Levy, @hannahmonica310, p. 4
Ian Sotomayor, @iansotomay (photo: Kelly Tran), p. 64
Iris Nicole Figues, @irisfigs, p. 91
Jana Sanchez, @waifwanderer, p. 15
Jason Chan, @jason_zyx, p. 76
Jesse, @kh_jesse0626, p. 43
Jessica Richards, @charlie_dog_in_LA, p. 62
John Allen Ampong, @_alien.foto_, p. 6
Jonathan Smith, @wanderlust.portraits, p. 60
Jorge Rivera, @jorgeshotthis, p. 86
Joseph Flores, @zheo_verticies, zheophotography.com, p. 24
Julianne Johnson, @julianne.jc, p. 57
Justin Pease, @itsjustinbitch, p. 21

Karol Franks, @okarol, flickr.com/photos/karolfranks, p. 45
Keegan Dunn, @keeganmdunn, keegandunnphotography.com, p. 72
Kellyn Kawaguchi, @theboldandvibrant, theboldandvibrant.com, p. 100
Kimberly Hicks, @kimberlydhicks, p. 26
Krista Blair, @kristaaablair, p. 33
Kristina M. Marshall, @kristina_marshall, p. 12
Kristina Moore, @sailorsushi, p. 96
Krystabel Manquiquis, @kbmangkeykeys, p. 8
Larissa Giampaoli, @roundtripweekend (@lallietand), roundtripweekend.com, p. 28
Laura Marquart, @blondiemonster (photo: Brian Maguire), p. 25
Lauren Natalia Kubota, @bon_mot_bot, p. 7
Lawrence Tai, @woodibly, p. 81
Leanne Marie Barrientos, @leeteaandpoetry, p. 92
Leigh Poindexter, @poindexterity, p. 53
Lerissa Gianchand, @________leri, p. 44
Lucas Passmore, @lucaspassmore, lucaspassmore.com, p. 10
Madelaine Fordham, @smaddielope, p. 74
Marielle Cabatingan, @macdaddymarmar, p. 75
Mary Hakimeh, @foodie_mary, p. 102
Melissa Brodsky, @melbrods (@sarah_witt1), p. 77
Melissa Hockings, @melissahockings, p. 55
Michael Traynor, @mjtraynor, p. 97
Molly Lichten Photography, @mmmols, mollylichten.com, p. 22
Nancy Gordy, @nancygordy, p. 58
Nazneen Shaik, @eazynazy, eazynazy.com, p. 71
Neal Hruby, @date.the.city, datethecity.com, p. 90
Nick Pes, @nickpes, nickpes.com, p. 27
Nicodemus Bernard, @nicpitre, visionarybrandsllc.com, p. 82
Oliver Kowalski, @oliver_kowalsky, p. 47
Otakar Senkyr, @insta.otakar, p. 41
Paul Andrew, @ppaulyo, 88
Peiwei Zhang, @peiwayfarer (photo: David Vasquez), p. 5
Peri Encinas, @periencinas, p. 50
Pretty in Pasadena, @prettyinpasadena (photo: Walter Simonsen & Taylor Mize), prettyinpasadena.com, p. 36
Rebecca King, @rebeccakooking (photo: Oliver English, olivertenglish.com), p. 101
R.J. Aguiar, @damnitrj, rjaguiar.com, p. 14
Roberto Solis Jr., @bertosolis, p. 49
Salina Mendoza, @salinamendozaart, salinamendoza.com, p. 70
Sara Diamond, @sara_diamond, saradiamond.com, p. 80
Sévanna Dias, @sevanna_ds (photo: Oceane Dias), p. 39
Shay Jiles, @theprinceandthep, theprinceandthep.com, p. 65
Skye Atwood, @skyeautumnwellness, p. 69
Small Forward, @smallforwardmusic (photo: Hannah Erskine), smallforward.bandcamp.com, p. 40
Tamara Daniel, @tamara_samira, p. 31
Tamara Melkonjan, @tomelkon, p. 18
Teresa Chang, @teresa.ctw (photo: Tingwei Chang), p. 61
Tina Li, @tinahli, inthecloudsevents.com, p. 63
Veronica E. Lo, @buenobassets, facebook.com/buenobassets.5, p. 13

Index

Note: Listings in bold are the official names of the Instagrammable spots.

Ace Hotel (DTLA), 80
Americana, The, 81
Angel City Brewery, 82
Angel Wings, 60
Angels Flight Railway, 40
Arcadia, 37, 53
ArcLight Hollywood, 23
Arlington Garden, 5
Arroyo Seco, 45
ArtCenter College of Design, 72
Artist & Craftsman Supply, 70
Arts District, 82
Ascot Hills Park, 6
Assembly Los Angeles wall, 61

Banksy, 70
Barnsdall Art Park, 7
Beverly Hills, 41, 56, 83
Beverly Hills Hotel, The, 83
Beverly Hills Sign, 41
Bill Rosendahl Memorial Lifeguard Tower, 77
Blade Runner, 57
Blue Ribbon Garden, 38
BonaVista Lounge, 103
Bradbury Building, 42
Broad, The, 20
Brunt, Michael, 77
Burbank, 91
Burden, Chris, 67
Burlington Arcade, 84

California African American Museum, 11
California Dreamin' mural, 62
California Science Center, 11
CalTech, 22
Cangelosi, Dominic, 95
Canter's Deli, 85
Capitol Records, 43
Carrey, Corinne, 69
Castle Green, 50
Chinatown Plaza, 44
Choi, Roy, 93
Christensen Alley, 50
Cinerama Dome, 23
Cisco Home, 68
Clifton's Republic, 86
Clockers' Corner, 37
Colorado Street Bridge, 45
Craft and Folk Art Museum, 21

Dark Knight Rises, The, 57
Degas, Edgar, 34
Dodger Stadium, 19
Dots Cafe mural, 63
DTLA, 20, 29, 30, 32, 35, 38, 40, 42, 44, 46, 57, 76, 79, 80, 82, 86, 88, 92, 97, 102, 103
Duran, Gonzalo, 71

Eastern Columbia Building, 46
Eaton Canyon waterfall, 8
Echo Park Lake, 9
Egyptian Theatre, 39
El Capitan Theatre, 39
El Matador State Beach, 10
Elliott Smith mural, 64
Elysian Park, 15
Exposition Park Rose Garden, 11

Fair Oaks Pharmacy, 87
Fairey, Shepard, 75
Fairfax High School, 94
Figure 8 (album), 64
Flower District, 88
Fork in the Road, 5
Frey, Viola, 50
Frontier Works, 79

Garland, Judy, 27
Gehry, Frank, 38
Getty, The, 24
Girls Tour wall, 65
Glendale, 33, 81, 95
Glendale Galleria, The, 81
Gosling, Ryan, 45
Gouveia, Geoff, 63
Grand Central Market, 79
Graval, Kelly, 72
Greenway Arts Alliance, 94
Griffith Observatory, 47
Griffith Park, 4, 47
Griffith, Griffith J., 47
Grove, The, 81

Harrison, George, 27
Henniger Flats, 8
Heritage Square Museum, 25
Hermosa Beach, 31, 66
Hermosa Beach murals, 66
Hidden Treasures, 89
Highland Park Bowl, 90
Hollyhock House, 7
Hollywood Boulevard, 39
Hollywood Bowl, 26
Hollywood Forever Cemetery, 27
Hollywood Sign, 48
Horowitz, Cher, 41
Huntington Library, Art Collections and Botanical Gardens, The, 3

In-N-Out, 91
Infinity Room, 20
Inglewood, 98
InterContinental Los Angeles Downtown, 74

Kaye, London, 59
Kendall, Kenneth, 47
Korean Bell of Friendship, 28
Koreatown, 93
Kusama, Yayoi, 20